JANICE VANCLEAVE

FIRST-PLACE SCIENCE FAIR PROJECTS™

STEP-BY-STEP
SCIENCE EXPERIMENTS IN

ASTRONOMY

rosen publishing's
rosen central®

NEW YORK

This edition first published in 2013 by:

The Rosen Publishing Group, Inc.
29 East 21st Street
New York, NY 10010

Library of Congress Cataloging-in-Publication Data

VanCleave, Janice Pratt.
Step-by-step science experiments in astronomy/Janice VanCleave.
    p. cm.—(Janice Vancleave's first-place science fair projects)
Includes bibliographical references and index.
ISBN 978-1-4488-6978-7 (lib. bdg.)—ISBN 978-1-4488-8461-2 (pbk.)—
ISBN 978-1-4488-8462-9 (6-pack)
1. Astronomy—Experiments—Juvenile literature.
2. Science projects—Juvenile literature. I. Title.
QB46.V364 2013
520.78—dc23

2012000715

Manufactured in the United States of America

CPSIA Compliance Information: Batch #S12YA: For further information, contact Rosen Publishing, New York, New York, at 1-800-237-9932.

This edition published by arrangement with and permission of John Wiley & Sons, Inc., Hoboken, New Jersey.

Originally published as *Astronomy For Every Kid.* Copyright © 1991 by John Wiley & Sons, Inc.

CONTENTS

INTRODUCTION

Astronomy is the study of celestial bodies, or objects in space such as planets and our Sun. This science includes information about the planet we live on—Earth—and all our neighbors in space. Studying astronomy, like all sciences, is a way of solving problems and discovering why celestial bodies behave the way they do.

Since ancient times, humans have been interested in the world around them. Shepherds spent their evenings viewing the ever-changing night sky. The stories about the imaginary figures in the heavens based on the constellations are still being told and enjoyed today.

Some of the earliest known astronomers were the Egyptians. About 5000 BCE, the Egyptians believed their valley—the Nile Valley—to be the lower boundary for the entire universe. The mountains surrounding the land were thought to be holding up the sky with its fixed stars that could be touched if one could climb to the top of one of the mountains. The sun god rode across the sky on a large barge each day and returned behind the mountains each night.

These early astronomers were forming the best conclusions from the facts available to them. As time passed, each generation gathered new information. New knowledge about the universe kept on correcting the false ideas of fixed stars and riding sun gods.

Early Egyptians and Chinese used their eyes to study the patterns of the sky carefully enough to make accurate calendars. During the second century CE, the Egyptian astronomer Ptolemy formulated his geocentric (Earth-centered) model of the universe, now known as the Ptolemaic system. It wasn't until the 1500s that the Polish astronomer Nicolaus Copernicus determined that Ptolemy's notion that the Sun revolved around Earth was invalid—instead, he concluded that Earth and the other planets actually orbited the Sun.

But there was no way to prove Copernicus's idea until the invention of the telescope. This revolutionary piece of technology allowed Italian astronomer Galileo Galilei in the early 1600s to carefully record the movement of different heavenly bodies, including four moons that he observed revolving around Jupiter. Galileo's findings paved the way for the confirmation of Copernicus's theory. Over time, telescopes became larger and more powerful. Now there are even telescopes in space. NASA's Kepler space telescope recently revealed a rocky planet, named Kepler-10b, that astronomers say is the smallest planet ever discovered outside our solar system.

In the twentieth century, scientists deepened their understanding not only of astronomy but also cosmology, the study of the universe and its laws. Along with technology, scientists used mathematics and physics to make discoveries. Albert Einstein revolutionized cosmology in 1905 with his special theory of relativity, which states that space and time can be seen as parts of a deeper structure, space-time, and that mass and energy are really the same thing. Scientists later developed the big bang theory. According to this theory, the universe started some thirteen billion years ago with a sudden expansion of matter and antimatter. Many scientific tests have confirmed the validity of this theory.

In this book, you will learn that astronomy is one of the few sciences in which amateurs can play a significant role. You don't need your own Hubble telescope or a Ph.D. in physics to make a significant contribution. With the proper tools—including knowledge and a sharp eye—even an amateur can make an important discovery. In 1995 two amateur astronomers, Alan Hale and Thomas Bopp, working independently of each other, discovered a comet beyond the orbit of Jupiter. Comet Hale-Bopp, as it came to be known, reached perihelion (closest distance to the Sun) on April 1, 1997, without ever coming very close to Earth. It was, however, spectacularly visible to the naked eye and became perhaps the most widely witnessed comet of the twentieth century.

Astronomy is more than stories about the constellations, the order of the planets, and how many moons or rings they might have. It is a study of how your life is affected by the things on and beyond Earth's atmosphere as well as how celestial bodies affect each other. Each of these science fair astronomy experiments has several sections: purpose, materials, step-by-step instructions and illustrations, expected results, and a scientific explanation in understandable terms.

The introductory purpose for each experiment gives a clue to the concept that will be introduced. The purpose is complete enough to present the goal but does not give away the mystery of the results.

Materials are needed, but in all the experiments the necessary items are easily obtained. Most of the materials are readily available around the house. A list of the necessary supplies is given for each experiment.

Detailed step-by-step instructions are given along with illustrations. The experiments are safe, and they work.

Expected results are used to direct the experimenter further. They provide immediate positive reinforcement and help answer any questions if the desired result isn't achieved.

Another special feature of the book is the "Why?" section, which gives a scientific explanation for each result in terms that are easily understood.

This book was written to provide you with safe, workable astronomy experiments. Its objective is to make the learning of what happens in the subject of astronomy a rewarding experience. It will help you to make the most of the exciting scientific era in which we live. It will guide you in discovering answers to questions such as: What is a barycenter? How does a telescope work? When is Neptune farther from the Sun than Pluto? The answers to these questions and many more will be discovered by performing the fun, safe, and workable experiments in this book.

Much information has been gathered about celestial bodies, but we have barely scratched the surface of the knowledge yet to be uncovered.

BENT

PURPOSE: To demonstrate how the thickness of an atmosphere affects the bending of light.

MATERIALS:

- 2 drinking cups
- 2 shiny pennies
- modeling clay, 2 grape-sized pieces

PROCEDURE:

1. Stick the pieces of clay in the inside bottom of each cup.

2. Press a penny in the clay so that it is in the very center of the cup. Do this in both cups.

2

3. Fill one cup with water.

4. Place both cups on the edge of a table. The cups must be side by side and even with the edge of the table.

5. Stand close to the table.

6. Take some steps backward while observing the pennies in the cups.

7. Stop when you can no longer see the pennies in either cup.

RESULTS The penny in the cup filled with air disappears from view first, while you can still see the penny in the cup filled with water.

WHY? You see the penny in the water at a greater distance because light enters the cup, reflects from the penny, hits the surface of the water, and is bent at an angle (refracted) toward your eye. The water is thicker than the air, and thicker materials refract the light more. A change in the thickness of Earth's atmosphere due to pollution increases the refraction of light. Venus's thick atmosphere refracts light much more than does Earth's atmosphere. An observer on Venus would see many mirages and distortions because of this.

BLUE SKY

PURPOSE: To determine why Earth is called the blue planet.

MATERIALS:

- flashlight
- drinking glass
- eye dropper
- milk
- spoon

PROCEDURE:

1. In a darkened room, shine the flashlight through the glass of water.

2. Add 1 drop of milk to the water and observe the light on the wall.

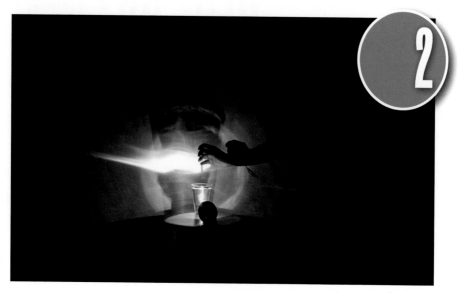

3. Turn on the lights in the room and stir the water.

4. Again, shine the light through the water.

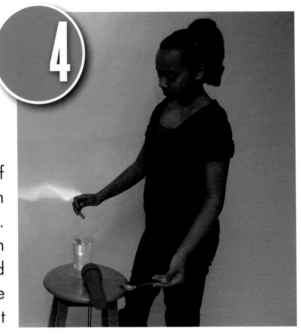

RESULTS The light passes through the clear water, but the milky water has a pale blue-gray look.

WHY? The waves of color in white light each have a different size. The particles of milk in the water separate and spread the small blue waves from the light throughout the water, causing the water to appear blue. Nitrogen and oxygen molecules in Earth's atmosphere, like the milk particles, are small enough to separate out the small blue light waves from sunlight. The blue light spreads out through the atmosphere, making the sky look blue from Earth and giving the entire planet a blue look when it is observed from space. The color in the glass is not a bright blue because more than just the blue light waves are being scattered by large particles in the milk. This happens in the atmosphere when large quantities of dust or water vapor scatter more than just the blue light waves. Clean, dry air produces the deepest blue sky color because the blue waves in the light are scattered the most.

BACK UP

PURPOSE: To demonstrate the apparent backward motion of Mars.

MATERIALS:

- helper

PROCEDURE:

1. Find a safe open space outside.

2. Ask a helper to stand next to you and then to slowly start walking forward.

3. Look past your helper's head and notice the background objects that he or she passes.

4. Start walking toward your helper at a faster speed than your helper.

5. Continue to observe the background past your helper's head.

6. Stop and ask your helper to stop when you are about 10 feet (3 m) in front of him or her.

RESULTS At first, you are looking forward to view the background past your helper, but as you take the lead you must look backward to see your helper and the objects beyond.

WHY? Your helper is not going backward; you are simply looking from a different position. Mars was thought by early observers to move forward, stop, go backward, and then go forward again. Actually the planet was continuing forward on its orbit around the Sun while Earth was zipping around the Sun in one-half the time of Mars's trip. Earth speeds ahead of Mars during part of the time, giving Mars the appearance of moving backward. Mars appears to move forward when Earth races around the orbit and approaches Mars from behind. This apparent change in the direction of Mars is called retrograde motion.

SEE THROUGH

PURPOSE: To determine how Saturn can be seen through its rings.

MATERIALS:

- ruler
- white poster board
- black marking pen
- scissors
- straight pin
- pencil
- glue

PROCEDURE:

1. Cut 3 strips from the poster board that are each 1 in. × 6 in. (2.5 cm × 15 cm).

2. Evenly space the strips so that their centers cross.

3. Glue the centers of the strips together.

4. Use the marking pen to make two marks across the end of each strip. Start the first mark ½ in. (1 cm) from the end of the strip and make the second mark 1 in. (2.5 cm) from the end.

5. Insert the pin through the center of the strips. Work the pin to enlarge the hole so that the paper blades easily spin.

6. Stick the end of the pin in a pencil eraser.

7. Spin the paper blades.

8. Observe the spinning blades.

RESULTS Two black rings are seen, but you can see through the spinning blades.

WHY? Your eyes blend the color on the paper strips together as they spin, producing what appears to be solid rings. The rings around Saturn are not solid, but their movement makes them appear to be a continuous surface as does the movement of the black marks on the spinning paper. Saturn's rings are made of ice chunks and pieces of rock that range in size from house-size pieces to those as small as the head of a pin. The surface of Saturn is seen through the spaces between the spinning ice and rock chunks, just as you were able to see through the spaces between the paper as it turned.

CURVES

PURPOSE: To demonstrate the effect of forces on orbital movement.

MATERIALS:

- pencil
- 2 chairs
- yardstick (meter stick)
- string
- small paper cup
- masking tape
- scissors
- salt
- poster board (dark color)

PROCEDURE:

1. Separate the chairs and tape the ends of the yardstick to the top edge of each chair's back.

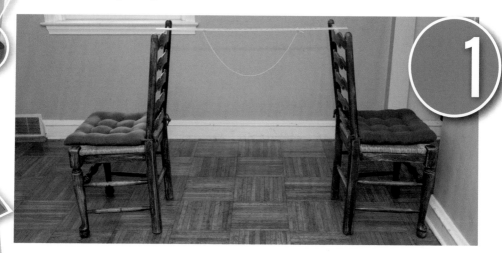

2. Cut two 1-yd. (1-m) lengths of string.

3. Attach both ends of one string to the yardstick to form a V-shaped support. Secure the ends with tape.

4. Loop the second string over the V-shaped string and use tape to attach the ends to the top rim of the cup, one on each side of the cup. Tie so that the cup is about 4 in. (10 cm) from the floor.

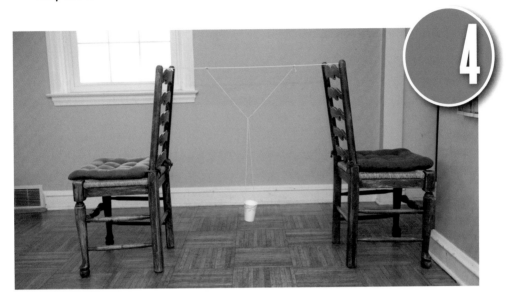

5. Lay the poster board under the hanging cup.

6. Fill the cup with salt.

7. Use the point of a pencil to make a small hole in the bottom of the cup.

8. Pull the cup back and release to allow it to swing forward.

RESULTS The falling salt forms different patterns on the dark paper as the cup swings.

WHY? The cup moves in different patterns because of the forces pulling on the cup. The cup was swung in a back and forth motion, the V-shaped support string pulled it in another direction, and there is the ever-present downward pull of gravity. Planets, like the cup, have different forces acting on them. Each planet spins on its axis and has a forward speed and is pulled on by other planets and its own moon(s), but the big pull is from the Sun. The combination of all of these forces guides the planet in the path (orbit) it takes around the Sun.

SPEEDY

PURPOSE: To determine the effect of distance on the orbiting speed of planets.

MATERIALS:
- 1 metal washer
- string

PROCEDURE:

Note: This activity is to be performed in an open, outside area away from other people.

1. Tie the washer to the end of a 1-yd. (1-m) length of string.
2. Hold the end of the string and extend your arm outward.

3. Swing your arm around so that the washer moves in a circular path beside your body.

4. Spin the washer at the slowest speed necessary to keep the string taut.

5. Hold the string in the center and again spin the washer at the slowest speed necessary to keep the string taut.

6. Hold the string about 10 in. (25 cm) from the washer and spin as before.

RESULTS As the length of the string decreases, the washer must be spun around more times in order to keep the string taut.

WHY? The washer seems to sluggishly move around in its circular path when attached to a long string, while on a shorter string, it zips around quickly. This slower and faster movement is real for planets that differ in their distance from the Sun. As the planet's distance from the Sun increases, the pull toward the Sun, called gravity, decreases. With less pull toward the Sun, the orbiting speed of the planet decreases. Mercury, the closest planet to the Sun, has the fastest orbiting speed, and Pluto, the further-most planet, has the very slowest orbiting speed. (Twirling the washer on the string is not a true simulation of how planets move around the Sun because the planets are not attached to the Sun by a cord.)

ON THE MOVE

PURPOSE: To determine why planets continue to move.

MATERIALS:

- round cake pan
- 1 sheet construction paper
- scissors
- 1 marble

PROCEDURE:

1. Use the cake pan to draw a circle on the paper.

1

2. Cut out the circle.

3. Place the pan on a flat surface.

4. Lay the paper inside the pan and place the marble on top of the paper.

5. Tap the marble so that it rolls around next to the wall of the pan.

6. Remove the paper from the pan.

7. Again tap the marble so that it rolls around next to the wall of the pan.

RESULTS The marble rolls in a circular path. It rolls farther and faster without the paper lining in the pan.

WHY? Inertia is the resistance that an object has to any change in its motion. Inertia causes stationary objects to remain at rest and moving objects to continue to move in a straight line, unless some force acts on them. All objects have inertia. The marble has much less inertia than do larger objects such as celestial bodies like the Sun, the Moon, and planets, but they all resist a change in motion. The marble stopped moving quicker in the paper-lined pan because of friction (the rubbing of one object against another). When the friction between the pan and the marble was reduced, the marble rolled for a longer time. The planets continue to move around the Sun because their movement through space is not restricted by friction.

SPINNER

PURPOSE: To determine why planets move smoothly around the Sun.

MATERIALS:

- ruler
- scissors
- heavy, thick string
- 4 large paper clips
- cardboard
- sheet of paper
- cake pan, 10-in. (25-cm) diameter
- pencil

PROCEDURE:

1. Use the cake pan to draw a circle on the paper and the cardboard.
2. Cut out the circles.

2

3. Fold the paper in half twice to find the center of the circle.

4. Lay the paper over the cardboard circle and make a hole through the center of both circles with the point of a pencil.

5. Discard the paper.

6. Cut a 1-yd. (1-m) length of string.

7. Thread one end of the string through the hole in the cardboard circle, and tie a knot on the other side to keep it from pulling back through.

8. Evenly space the 4 paper clips around the outer rim of the cardboard circle or disk.

9. Hold the end of the string and swing the disk back and forth.

10. Continue to hold the end of the string while you give the disk a quick spin toward you, then swing it as before.

RESULTS The disk flops around when merely moved around on the string, but when spun, it rotates in the plane in which it was originally spun.

WHY? The cardboard disk acts like a gyroscope, a kind of top which when spinning stays pointed in one direction. The planets spin on their axis as they rotate around the Sun. This keeps them turning in the plane in which they were started just as the disk does.

HOW FAR?

PURPOSE: To demonstrate how Neptune moves farther from the Sun than Pluto.

MATERIALS:

- tack board
- 6 push tacks
- string
- pencil
- scissors
- ruler
- paper

PROCEDURE:

1. Cut a piece of string 12 in. (30 cm) long.

2. Tie the ends of the string together to form a loop that is about 6 in. (18 cm) long.

3. Secure a piece of paper to the tack board with 4 tacks.

4. Draw a line 5 in. (13 cm) long and stick a tack in each end of the line.

5. Position the loop of string around the tacks.

6. Place the pencil so that its point is against the inside of the loop.

7. Keep the string taut as you guide the pencil around the inside of the string to draw an oval or ellipse on the paper.

8. Cut an 8-in. (20-cm) length of string and tie the ends together to form a loop.

9. Move the tacks and make new drawings until a position is found that produces a small ellipse inside the larger one with one end of the small ellipse overlapping the larger one.

RESULTS Two overlapping elliptical orbits are drawn.

WHY? The orbits of all planets have an elliptical shape. Pluto's orbit overlaps the orbit of Neptune. It takes Pluto 248 years to make one trip around the Sun. During the journey, Pluto moves inside Neptune's orbit, making Neptune's orbit farther than that of Pluto. Pluto last reached its perihelion (the point closest to the Sun) in 1989.

BALANCING POINT

PURPOSE: To demonstrate the position of Earth's barycenter.

MATERIALS:

- scissors
- string
- modeling clay
- pencil
- ruler

PROCEDURE:

1. Cut a 12-in. (30-cm) length of string.

2. Tie the string about 1 in. (3 cm) from the end of the pencil.

3. Make a ball of clay, about the size of a lemon.

4. Stick the clay ball on the end of the pencil with the string.

35

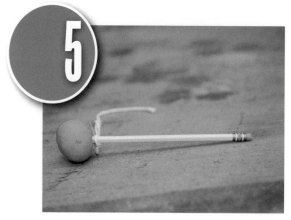

5. Mold the clay around the string so that the string is barely inside the edge of the clay ball.

6. Add a grape-sized piece of clay to the opposite end of the pencil.

7. Hold the end of the string and add small pieces of clay to the end of the pencil. It may take several tries but keep doing this until the pencil balances horizontally.

RESULTS The pencil hangs in a horizontal position.

WHY? The string is tied at the center of gravity—the point at which the weight of an object is evenly placed. Objects can be balanced at their center of gravity. The Moon and Earth move around the Sun like a single body. The center of gravity of the Earth-Moon system is called the barycenter. The barycenter is about 1,044 miles (1,670 km) beneath Earth's surface on the side of Earth facing the Moon. The string represents Earth's barycenter on the Earth-Moon model.

SATELLITE CRASH

PURPOSE: To demonstrate why a satellite stays in orbit.

MATERIALS:

- large, empty, 3-lb. (1.4-kg) coffee can
- poster board
- pencil
- scissors
- glass marble
- masking tape

PROCEDURE:

1. On the poster board, draw a circle with a 22 in. (55 cm) diameter.

2. Cut around the circle, then cut out a wedge (pie slice) that is one-eighth of the circle.

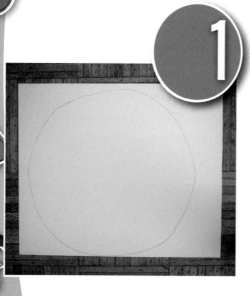

3. Overlap the circle to form a cone that fits snugly in the coffee can with most of the cone sticking out the top of the can. Tape the cone so it does not open up.

4. Tape the cone to the outside of the can.

5. Roll the marble around the top of the cone as fast as possible and observe its movement.

RESULTS The marble rolls around the inside of the cone and its path begins to curve downward as the speed of the marble slows. The marble finally moves to the bottom of the cone and stops.

WHY? The paper offers a continuous resistance to the movement of the marble, forcing it to move in a circular path, and gravity pulls the marble downward. As the forward speed of the marble decreases, the unchanging pull of gravity forces the marble to move down the cone toward the bottom. Satellites would continue to circle Earth if they never lost their forward motion, but like the marble, as their speed decreases, gravity pulls them toward Earth until finally they crash into Earth. Planets and moons are examples of satellites since they all orbit another celestial body; they would crash if their forward speed decreased.

IN AND OUT

PURPOSE: To demonstrate forces that keep satellites in orbit.

MATERIALS:

- masking tape
- metal spoon
- thread spool
- string
- yardstick (meter stick)

PROCEDURE:

1. Cut 1 yd. (1 m) of string.
2. Tie one end of the string to the roll of tape.
3. Thread the free end of the string through the hole in the spool.
4. Tie the spoon to the free end of the string.

41

5. Hold the tape in one hand and hold the spoon with your free hand.

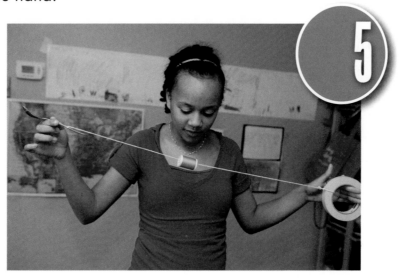

6. Give the spool a quick circular motion to start it spinning in a horizontal circle above your head.

7. Release the tape and allow it to hang freely.

8. Keep the spoon spinning by moving the thread spool in a circular motion.

9. Observe the movement of the tape roll.

RESULTS The spoon spins in a circular path with only the weight of the tape pulling on the attached string.

WHY? The tape pulls on the string and provides an inward force that keeps the spoon moving in a circular path. This force toward the center is called a centripetal force. Centripetal means center-seeking. If the force of the string were removed, the spoon would fly off in a straight line. Any circling object, spoon or satellite, has a centripetal force keeping it in its circular path. Moons that orbit planets and planets that orbit the Sun all are pulled toward the celestial body that they orbit. Their own forward speed keeps them from being pulled into the body that they orbit, and the centripetal force acting on the orbiting body keeps it from moving off into space.

13 SUN CAMERA

PURPOSE: To determine the size of the Sun.

MATERIALS:

- 1 sheet of paper
- yardstick (meter stick)
- masking tape
- pencil
- 1 index card
- straight pin

PROCEDURE:

1. Draw two parallel lines on the sheet of paper about the thickness of the pencil lead apart.

2. Punch a hole in the center of the index card with the straight pin.

3. Fold one edge of the card and tape the folded edge to the zero end of the yardstick.

4. Hold the paper at the 8½-in. (218-mm) mark.

5. Stand so that the shadow of the card falls on the paper.

6. Look carefully at the paper and locate the small circle of light. (Caution: NEVER look directly into the Sun because it can damage your eyes.)
7. Move the paper so that the circle of light fills the space between the lines on the sheet.

RESULTS The image of the Sun fits between the parallel lines on the paper.

WHY? The distance from the hole in the card to the paper is 109 times the width (diameter) of the circle of light on the paper. Dividing the distance from the hole in the card to the paper by 109 will result in the diameter of the circle.

- distance ÷ 109 = diameter
- 8½ in. ÷ 109 = thickness of the pencil lead
- 218 mm ÷ 109 = 2 mm

The distance from Earth to the Sun is 109 times the Sun's diameter. Astronomers have determined the distance from Earth to the Sun to be about 93,750,000 miles (150,000,000 km). Dividing the distance to the Sun by 109 will give the diameter of the Sun:

- distance ÷ 109 = diameter
- 93,750,000 mi. ÷ 109 = 86,009 mi. (137,614.4 km)

FACE FORWARD

PURPOSE: To demonstrate that the Moon rotates on its axis.

MATERIALS:

- 2 sheets of paper
- marker
- masking tape

PROCEDURE:

1. Draw a circle in the center of one sheet of paper.

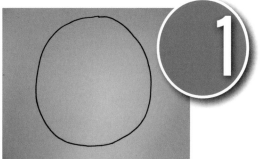

2. Write the word "Earth" in the center of the circle, and place the paper on the floor.

3. Mark a large X in the center of the second sheet of paper, and tape this paper to a wall.

4. Stand by the side of the paper on the floor and face the X on the wall.

5. Walk around "Earth," but continue to face the X.
6. Next, turn so that you face the paper labeled "Earth."
7. Walk around "Earth," but continue to face it.

RESULTS Facing the X-marked paper resulted in different parts of your body pointing toward the paper marked "Earth" as you revolved around it. Continuing to face "Earth" allowed only your front side to point toward it during the revolution.

WHY? You had to turn your body slightly in order to continue to face "Earth" as you moved around it. In order for the same side of the Moon to always face Earth, the Moon also has to turn slowly on its axis as it moves around Earth. The Moon rotates one complete turn on its own axis during the 28 days it takes to revolve around Earth.

15 HEAVY

PURPOSE: To demonstrate the effect of the Moon's gravity on weight.

MATERIALS:
- marker
- masking tape
- 2 rubber bands
- string
- large rock
- large cooking pot or bucket
- string
- scissors

PROCEDURE:

1. Tie the rubber bands together.

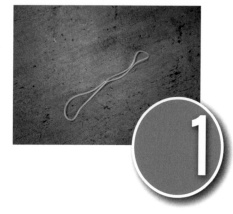

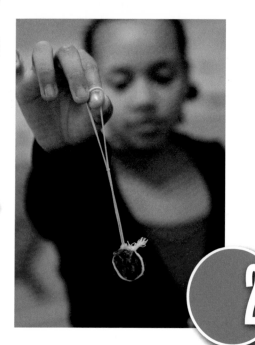

2. Tie a string around the rock and attach the string to the rubber bands.

3. Place the cooking pot on a table.

4. Set the rock in the bottom of the pot.

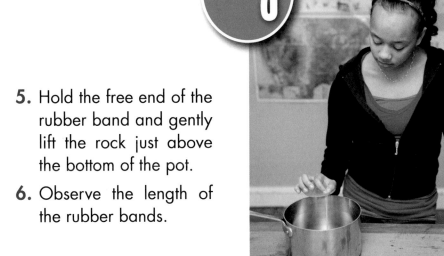

5. Hold the free end of the rubber band and gently lift the rock just above the bottom of the pot.

6. Observe the length of the rubber bands.

7. Fill the pot with water.

8. Set the rock in the pot.
9. Hold the rubber band and lift the rock just above the bottom of the pot.
10. Observe the length of the rubber bands.

RESULTS The length of the rubber bands needed to support the rock decreased when water was poured into the pot.

WHY? Gravity pulls down on the rock, causing the attached rubber bands to stretch. Adding water to the pot decreases the downward pull. The water pushes up on the rock, canceling some of the downward pull of gravity. The pull of gravity through the water simulates the reduced gravity on our Moon. The rubber bands would stretch even less if the rock were picked up on Moon because the Moon's gravity is only one-sixth that of the Earth's gravity.

DISTANT STARS

PURPOSE: To determine which star is closest to Earth.

MATERIALS:
- your thumb
- modeling clay
- pencil

PROCEDURE:

1. Use the modeling clay to hold the pencil in a vertical position on a table.

2. Stand across the room and hold your thumb at arm's length in front of your face.

3. Close your left eye.
4. Using your right eye, look across the tip of your thumb at the pencil eraser.

5. Do not move your head or your thumb. Close your right eye and use your left eye to look at the tip of your thumb.

6. Notice the distance your thumb seems to move when you switch eyes.
7. Hold your thumb at the end of your nose and again use your right eye to look across the tip of your thumb at the pencil eraser.

8. Do not move your thumb or your head. Look at your thumb tip with your left eye. Notice how far your thumb seems to move in relation to the pencil.

RESULTS Switching from the right to the left eye seems to make your thumb move. The movement is greater when your thumb is closer to the eyes.

WHY? Your thumb appears to move because it is being viewed from different angles. The movement is greatest when your thumb is closest to the face. A star close to Earth has an apparent change in its position when viewed from different sides of Earth's orbit. During the winter, an observer from Earth would see star A behind the close star, but during the summer, star B appears behind the close star. This is because the close star is being viewed from different angles; this apparent movement is called stellar parallax. When comparing the stellar parallax of two different stars, the one that seems to move the most will be the star closer to Earth.

BOX PLANETARIUM

PURPOSE: To demonstrate how planetariums produce images of the night sky.

MATERIALS:

- shoe box
- black construction paper
- cellophane tape
- flashlight
- straight pin
- scissors

PROCEDURE:

1. Cut a square from the end of the shoe box.

2. At the other end of the box, cut a circle just large enough to insert the end of the flashlight.

3. Cover the square opening with a piece of black paper. Secure the paper to the box with tape.

4. Use the pin to make 7 to 8 holes in the black paper.
5. Point the shoebox toward a blank wall.
6. In a darkened room, turn on the flashlight.

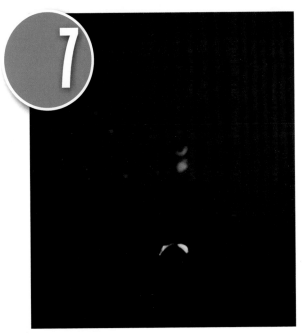

7. Move back and forth from the wall to form clear images of small light spots on the wall. Make the holes in the black paper larger if the spots on the wall are too small.

RESULTS An enlarged pattern of the holes made in the paper is projected onto the wall.

WHY? As light beams shine through the tiny holes, they spread outward, producing larger circles of light on the wall. A planetarium presentation showing the entire night sky uses a round sphere with holes spaced in the positions of single stars and constellations. A constellation is a group of stars whose arrangement forms an imaginary figure. A bright light in the center of the sphere projects light spots on a curved ceiling representing the sky. As the ball rotates, different star groups are seen. Because of Earth's revolution around the Sun, different stars are viewed in the sky at different times of the year.

STAR CHART

PURPOSE: To record the position of the Big Dipper and Polaris, the North Star.

MATERIALS:

- white poster paper
- string
- large nail
- marker
- helper

PROCEDURE:

1. Cut a string 12 in. (30 cm) longer than your height.
2. With an adult's assistance, tie one end of the string to a nail.

3. On a clear, moonless night, lay a sheet of white poster paper on the ground outside.

4. Stand on the edge of the paper and point to a star in the Big Dipper constellation while holding the free end of the string, allowing the nail to hang freely.

5. Ask a helper to mark a spot on the paper under the hanging nail.

6. Point to each of the stars in the Big Dipper as your helper marks their position on the paper.

7. Find and mark the position of the North Star by drawing a straight line from the first star in the bowl of the dipper to the star in the handle of Ursa Minor, the Little Dipper constellation.

RESULTS The position of part of the Ursa Major constellation called the Big Dipper is drawn on the paper, and Polaris, the North Star, is plotted on the star chart.

WHY? As your finger moves from one star to the next, the free hanging nail moves to a new position, thus plotting the position of the stars. Polaris, the star that Earth's imaginary axis points to, is also called the North Star. This star can be found by allowing the first star in the bowl of the Big Dipper to be the pointer star.

TWINKLING STAR

PURPOSE: To determine why stars twinkle.

MATERIALS:

- flashlight
- aluminum foil
- glass bowl, 2 qt. (2 liter)
- pencil

PROCEDURE:

1. Cut a piece of aluminum foil large enough to fit under the bowl. Wrinkle the piece of foil with your hands.

2. Fill the bowl half full with water and place it on top of the wrinkled piece of aluminum foil.

3. In a darkened room, hold the flashlight over the top of the bowl.

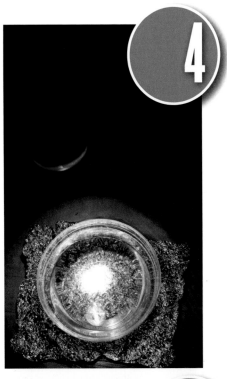

4. Observe the foil and take note of how it appears when viewed through undisturbed water.

5. Continue to shine the light through the water as you gently tap the surface of the water with a pencil.

6. Observe the foil as it appears when viewed through moving water.

RESULTS The moving water causes the light reflecting from the aluminum foil to blur.

WHY? Light travels in a straight line, and the waves on the water's surface cause the light rays to leave in different directions. This change in the direction of light rays is called refraction. Other light sources, such as stars, behave in the same manner when the light passes through moving material. A star appears to twinkle when viewed from Earth because the star's light passes through layers of moving air before reaching the viewer's eyes. The light is bent this way and that as it moves through whirling packets of air in Earth's atmosphere. The scientific term for twinkling is scintillation. Stars do not scintillate when viewed from a spacecraft above Earth's atmosphere because there is not enough material in space to refract the star's light.

UP OR DOWN?

PURPOSE: To demonstrate how light travels through the lens of a refractive telescope.

MATERIALS:

- goose-neck desk lamp
- magnifying lens
- dark construction paper, 1 sheet
- scissors
- masking tape

PROCEDURE:

1. Cut a paper circle from the dark paper to fit the opening of the lamp.

2. Cut an arrow design in the center of the paper circle.

3. Tape the circle over the lamp.

4. Caution: Be sure that the paper does not rest on the light bulb. The bulb will get hot.

5. Place the lamp about 6 ft. (2 m) from a wall.

6. Darken the room with the exception of the lamp.

7. Hold the magnifying lens about 12 in. (30 cm) from the lamp.

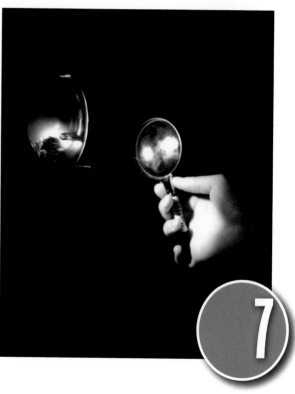

8. Move the magnifying lens back and forth from the lamp until a clear image is projected on the wall.

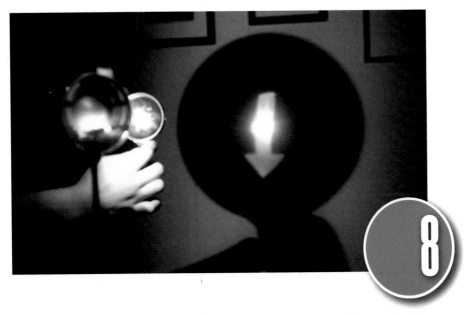

RESULTS The image produced on the wall is turned upside down.

WHY? Light travels in a straight line, but when it hits the lens, it changes direction, causing the image to be upside down. Refractive telescopes have lenses similar to the one used in this experiment, and so stars viewed through a refractive telescope appear upside down.

SIMPLE

PURPOSE: To demonstrate how a refracting telescope works.

MATERIALS:

- sheet of notebook paper
- 2 magnifying lenses

PROCEDURE:

1. Close one eye and look at an open window through one of the magnifying lenses.

1

2. Move the lens back and forth slowly until the objects outside the window are clearly in focus.

3. Without moving the lens, place a sheet of paper between you and the lens.

4. Move the paper back and forth until a clear image appears on the sheet.

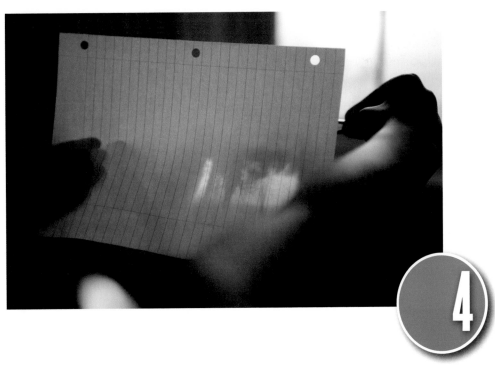

5. Replace the paper with the second lens.

6. Move the second lens back and forth to find the position where the image looks clear when looking through both lenses.

RESULTS A small, inverted image of the objects outside the window is projected onto the paper. The image seen through both lenses is upside down and larger than when seen through one lens.

WHY? The furthermost lens is called the objective lens. It collects light from the distant objects and brings it into focus. At the focal point, an image, or picture, of the object exists and can be projected onto a screen. The second lens, called the eyepiece lens, collects light from the image and brings an enlarged, inverted image into focus in front of your eyes.

BOUNCER

PURPOSE: To demonstrate how communication satellites work.

MATERIALS:
- flashlight
- flat mirror
- helper
- modeling clay

PROCEDURE:
1. Use the clay to stand the mirror on a table positioned near an open door.

2. Have a person stand in the next room so that he or she can see the mirror through the door, but not see you.

3. Shine the light on the surface of the mirror.

4. You and your helper need to find a position that allows the light to reflect from the mirror so that your helper sees the light.

RESULTS The light beam is sent from one room and seen by a person in another room.

WHY? The shiny surface of the mirror reflects the light. Radio waves, like the light, can be reflected from smooth surfaces and directed to receivers at different places around the world. A signal sent to an orbiting satellite is bounced back at an angle to a receiver many miles away from the sender.

GLOSSARY

barycenter Center of gravity between the Moon-Earth system, or point at which this system moves around the Sun.

celestial Relating to objects in space.

center of gravity The point at which the weight of an object is equally distributed. The object will balance at this point.

centripetal force The force pulling toward the center that keeps an object moving in a curved path.

constellation A group of stars that, viewed from Earth, form the outline of an object or figure.

elliptical Describing a closed curve with an oval shape.

friction The resistance created when rubbing one object against another.

gravity The attraction between two objects because of their mass. Earth pulls everything toward its center.

inertia Resistance to any sudden change in state, motion, or rest.

mirage An image of something that is not real.

orbit The path of an object around another body; planets moving around the Sun.

orbiting speed Rate that an object moves in a curved path; the speed of planets around the Sun.

perihelion Point in a planet's orbit when the planet is closest to the Sun.

radio waves Energy waves produced by charged particles that are naturally emitted by the Sun and other stars. They are produced by the motion of electrons in the antenna of broadcasting stations.

refraction The change of speed of light as it moves from one material into another.

retrograde The backward movement of an object, such as the apparent retrograde motion of Mars.

satellite A small object that circles a larger body.

scintillation Scientific term used to indicate the apparent twinkling of a star.

shadow Area where light is blocked by an object.

stellar parallax The difference in a star's apparent position when it is viewed from different angles.

Amateur Astronomers Association
P.O. Box 150253
Brooklyn, NY 11215
(212) 535-2922
Web site: http://www.aaa.org
The Amateur Astronomers Association is a nonprofit organization that unites and fosters amateur astronomers to
  continue their critical research and contribution to the
  science.

American Astronomical Society
2000 Florida Avenue NW, Suite 400
Washington, DC 20009-1231
(202) 328-2010
Web site: http://www.aas.org
The American Astronomical Society is an organization that
  brings together astronomers from around the world to
  keep them updated on the latest findings and develop-
  ments in the science.

American Physical Society
One Physics Ellipse
College Park, MD 20740-3844
(301) 209-3200
Web site: http://www.aps.org
The American Physical Society brings together the world's
  preeminent physicists and astronomers to share insights on
  the science of cosmology.

Hayden Planetarium
Department of Astrophysics
American Museum of Natural History
Central Park West at 79th Street
New York, NY 10024
(212) 769-5901
Web site: http://www.haydenplanetarium.org
Located in the American Museum of Natural History in New
    York, the Hayden Planetarium offers museum-goers a look
    at the night sky like they've never seen before.

NASA
Public Communications Office
NASA Headquarters
Suite 5K39
Washington, DC 20546-0001
(202) 358-0001
Web site: http://www.nasa.gov
NASA, or the National Aeronautics and Space
    Administration, is the agency of the United States govern-
    ment committed to space exploration and study.

Web Sites

Due to the changing nature of Internet links, Rosen Publishing has
developed an online list of Web sites related to the subject of this book.
This site is updated regularly. Please use this link to access the list:

http://www.rosenlinks.com/scif/astro

FOR FURTHER READING

Aguilar, David A. *13 Planets: the Latest View of the Solar System*. Washington, DC: National Geographic, 2011.

Croce, Nicholas. *Newton and the Three Laws of Motion*. New York: Rosen Pub. Group, 2005.

Dickinson, Terence. *NightWatch: A Practical Guide to Viewing the Universe*. Buffalo, NY: Firefly, 2006.

Greene, B. *The Fabric of the Cosmos: Space, Time, and the Texture of Reality*. New York, NY: Vintage, 2005.

Gribbin, John R., and Mary Gribbin. *From Here to Infinity: a Beginner's Guide to Astronomy*. New York, NY: Sterling, 2008.

Hawking, S. W., and Leonard Mlodinow. *A Briefer History of Time*. New York, NY: Bantam, 2008.

Hawking, S. W. *On the Shoulders of Giants: the Great Works of Physics and Astronomy*. Philadelphia, PA: Running, 2002.

Inglis, Mike. *Astrophysics Is Easy!: A Complete Introduction for Amateur Astronomers*. New York, NY: Springer, 2007.

Isaacson, Walter. *Einstein: His Life and Universe*. New York, NY: Simon & Schuster Paperbacks, 2008.

Kaku, Michio. *Physics of the Future: How Science Will Shape Human Destiny and Our Daily Lives by the Year 2100*. New York, NY: Doubleday, 2011.

Kaku, Michio. *Physics of the Impossible: A Scientific Exploration into the World of Phasers, Force Fields, Teleportation, and Time Travel*. New York, NY: Anchor, 2009.

Lippincott, Kristen. *Eyewitness Astronomy*. New York, NY: DK Publishing, 2008.

Moché, Dinah L. *Astronomy: a Self-Teaching Guide.*
    Hoboken, NJ: John Wiley, 2009.
Rhatigan, Joe, and Rain Newcomb. *Out-of-This-World
    Astronomy.* New York, NY: Lark, 2005.
Singh, Simon. *Big Bang: The Origin of the Universe.* New
    York, NY: Harper Perennial, 2005.
Sinnott, Roger W. *Sky & Telescope's Pocket Sky Atlas.*
    Cambridge, MA: Sky Pub., 2006.
Stott, Carole. *Space: From Earth to the Edge of the Universe.*
    New York, NY, NY: DK Publishing, 2010.

INDEX

About The Author

Janice VanCleave is a former school science teacher and a captivating presenter at museums, schools, and bookstores nationwide. She is the author of more than twenty other science books for children.

Designer: Nicole Russo; Editor: Nicholas Croce